Editor-in-Chief and Founder:
  Lyndon H. LaRouche, Jr.
Editorial Board: *Lyndon H. LaRouche, Jr. , Helga
  Zepp-LaRouche, Robert Ingraham, Tony
  Papert, Gerald Rose, Dennis Small, Jeffrey
  Steinberg, William Wertz*
Co-Editors: *Robert Ingraham, Tony Papert*
Managing Editor: *Nancy Spannaus*
Technology: *Marsha Freeman*
Books: *Katherine Notley*
Ebooks: *Richard Burden*
Graphics: *Alan Yue*
Photos: *Stuart Lewis*
Circulation Manager: *Stanley Ezrol*

INTELLIGENCE DIRECTORS
Counterintelligence: *Jeffrey Steinberg, Michele
  Steinberg*
Economics: *John Hoefle, Marcia Merry Baker,
  Paul Gallagher*
History: *Anton Chaitkin*
Ibero-America: *Dennis Small*
Russia and Eastern Europe: *Rachel Douglas*
United States: *Debra Freeman*

INTERNATIONAL BUREAUS
Bogotá: *Miriam Redondo*
Berlin: *Rainer Apel*
Copenhagen: *Tom Gillesberg*
Houston: *Harley Schlanger*
Lima: *Sara Madueño*
Melbourne: *Robert Barwick*
Mexico City: *Gerardo Castilleja Chávez*
New Delhi: *Ramtanu Maitra*
Paris: *Christine Bierre*
Stockholm: *Ulf Sandmark*
United Nations, N.Y.C.: *Leni Rubinstein*
Washington, D.C.: *William Jones*
Wiesbaden: *Göran Haglund*

ON THE WEB
e-mail: eirns@larouchepub.com
www.larouchepub.com
www.executiveintelligencereview.com
www.larouchepub.com/eiw
Webmaster: *John Sigerson*
Assistant Webmaster: *George Hollis*
Editor, Arabic-language edition: *Hussein Askary*

EIR (ISSN 0273-6314) *is published weekly
(50 issues), by EIR News Service, Inc.,
P.O. Box 17390, Washington, D.C. 20041-0390.
(703) 777-9451*

European Headquarters: E.I.R. GmbH, Postfach
Bahnstrasse 9a, D-65205, Wiesbaden, Germany
Tel: 49-611-73650
Homepage: http://www.eirna.com
e-mail: eirna@eirna.com
Director: Georg Neudecker

Montreal, Canada: 514-461-1557

Denmark: EIR - Danmark, Sankt Knuds Vej 11,
basement left, DK-1903 Frederiksberg, Denmark.
Tel.: +45 35 43 60 40, Fax: +45 35 43 87 57. e-mail:
eirdk@hotmail.com.

Mexico City: EIR, Sor Juana Inés de la Cruz 242-2
Col. Agricultura C.P. 11360
Delegación M. Hidalgo, México D.F.
Tel. (5525) 5318-2301
eirmexico@gmail.com

Canada Post Publication Sales Agreement
#40683579

Postmaster: Send all address changes to *EIR*, P.O.
Box 17390, Washington, D.C. 20041-0390.

Signed articles in *EIR* represent the views of the
authors, and not necessarily those of the Editorial
Board.

Putin's 'Greater Eurasia Project'

LAROUCHE

The British System Is Doomed: A Totally New System Is Now Urgent

Lyndon LaRouche offered an assessment of the current global situation in dialogue with colleagues on June 17. A paraphrase of his remarks follows.

The present British Empire trans-Atlantic financial system is hopelessly bankrupt and doomed to crash. While the date-certain of such a crash cannot be forecast, the inevitability of the crash is undeniable. No measures of reform or modification can work. There is no way to "manage" this imminent collapse. We are on the edge of an unpredictable blowout.

A thoroughly new system must be established, and it is now a priority that rational forces in the West take up this immediate challenge. This requires a thoroughly new approach, based upon well established principles of physical economy. Intelligent people must realize that speculation will not work. All of the existing gambling debt must be cancelled immediately. We must start all over, with a completely new approach. It is time to bring the dominant, now bankrupt British System to an end. The French System,— basically everything that has happened since the fall of President Charles DeGaulle,— must also be cast aside as a doomed failure.

The trans-Atlantic region must be put through a top-to-bottom reconstruction. There can be no deals with existing powers, who have brought the region to the edge of the greatest blowout in modern history.

We need to concentrate on creating a new system of physical values, measured in qualitative increases in the productive powers of labor, driven by scientific discoveries that have not yet even been conceptualized. Price values must be repudiated. Hamiltonian principles of physical economy, reflecting the new challenges and new scientific frontiers to be conquered, must be adopted.

This requires an entirely new mode of thinking, a genuinely new paradigm, based on the commitment to future generations and to the pursuit of new scientific discoveries that demonstrate man's unique capacity for creative discovery of the nature of the universe and man's relations within it.

Everything associated with the British System, every policy associated with the United States under Barack Obama, must be scrapped.

Among all of the world's leaders, Russian President Vladimir Putin has the best grasp of this critical moment. His perspective, most recently reflected in his statements at the St. Petersburg International Economic Forum, are unmatched. He understands that the greatest risk to mankind comes from the British and from Obama, who are the biggest threats, because they are devoted to defending the present doomed system of speculation, and they will risk global war—even global thermonuclear war—to defend that dead system.

EIR Contents

www.larouchepub.com Volume 43, Number 26, June 24, 2016

kremlin.ru

Cover This Week

12,000 people, 1,300 businesses attended the June 16-18 St. Petersburg International Economic Forum.

Our Task Today

Helga Zepp-LaRouche spoke to the following effect in concluding a telephone meeting with the LaRouche PAC Policy Committee, June 16.

The crucial thing is to mediate the historic tension of this moment, throughout our movement and beyond. The biggest danger would be for people to go on with business as usual, thinking that, well, we have always been saying there was a crisis. But right now, look at all the elements coming together: the war danger, the military maneuvers, the NATO summit, the fight to prolong the anti-Russian sanctions, the possibility of Britain's exit from the Euro, and with it the collapse of the financial system.

On the positive side, there's the St. Petersburg International Economic Forum, which will be attended by Italian Prime Minister Renzi, European Commission President Juncker, UN Secretary-General Ban Ki-Moon, and many CEOs and other leaders of governments,— so Russia is not isolated at all! Then Xi Jinping will come for a 5-day trip to Central Europe and Central Asia, starting with Poland June 17. There is all the progress around the Silk Road, integration, the Eurasian Economic Union, and ASEAN, as more train routes are also continuing to be opened between China and Europe.

All of this is moving forward, and the tension is: Which system will prevail? Will it be the global development partnership which is on the horizon and moving forward, or will the forces of the empire go for the annihilation of mankind? The tension between these two dynamics has never been as acute as right now. That's the sense we have to mediate. If they think it's just Orlando, or just this or just that,— then they don't understand it at all.

The reason that the Walter Jones initiative, House Resolution 779, is so important in this context, is because that could derail the whole British-Saudi foreign policy of the United States,— which is the crux of the matter. So, the Walter Jones resolution is an integral part of the initiative to change it, but people must not treat it as a single issue, but instead say that that's how you can do something to stop the war danger. And you have to learn how all of these things hang together.

And what we have to do as an organization, is to communicate that this is probably the most important *punctum saliens* in human history. And we have to elevate people onto the stage of strategic world-historical developments. That's why they have to join us, because they don't get that kind of view from anyone else,— but that's what they need to survive. That's the challenge which we have to communicate.

EIRNS/Stefan Tolksdorf

Helga Zepp-LaRouche introducing Chinese translation of EIR*'s Special Report,* The New Silk Road Becomes the World Land-Bridge.

Bending Stars Like Reeds Towards A New System of Extra-Planetary Value

by Michael G. Steger, LaRouche PAC Policy Committee

June 20—There is no going back.

The current British-dominated trans-Atlantic system is in the throes of destruction, chaos, and possible anarchy. There is no option of a non-collapse, as Lyndon LaRouche stated in July of 2007 when the housing bubble was set to blow a week later.

He said it again this past week,— yet this time, his emphasis was different.

This is not the collapse of a housing bubble, stock bubble, or banking system. This is the collapse of the whole system—a monetary death cult crowned with killer Obama, which has been cannibalizing the population of the trans-Atlantic regions incessantly since the death of Franklin Roosevelt in 1945. There is now nearly nothing left on which to feed.

The options are two: a new system of value and human development premised on mankind's travel among the stars, or the British Crown's scorched-earth policy that inevitably leads to nuclear annihilation as its ultimate act.

The path to long-term survival will be found not in formal procedures or symbolic schemes, but with the creative spirit and immortal courage of the likes of space pioneer Krafft Ehricke, a genius who first prevailed against the Nazis of Germany, then again over the fascists of the F.B.I., and then again over the satanic environmentalists, to demonstrate the triumphant immortal spirit of mankind's extraterrestrial imperative.

One More Day, Maybe One More Week

Consider an overview of the trans-Atlantic system.

Europe, under British-NATO control, is currently risking nuclear war with extensive and repeated military exercises along Russia's border, for the first time since the Nazi invasion. And while Russia patiently calls for collaborative efforts to address the growing danger of terrorism, Europe faces the greatest migration of peoples since before World War II, the result of a refugee crisis caused by the British-directed wars over the last fifteen years, all of which have been inflamed under Obama's color revolutions, his regime-changes, and his killer-drone program.

It is no surprise then, that every nation in Europe faces populist revolts in the wake of decades of political cowardice, and that now increasingly far right-wing and environmentalist political movements are surging, which echo the 1920s and 30s fascist uprisings.

U.S. Army/Pfc. Casey Dinnison

Polish soldiers on June 11, 2016, aiding a simulated casualty during NATO exercise Anakonda 2016, in Poland, which involved 31,000 participants from more than 20 countries. Other NATO exercises have involved over 30,000 more troops.

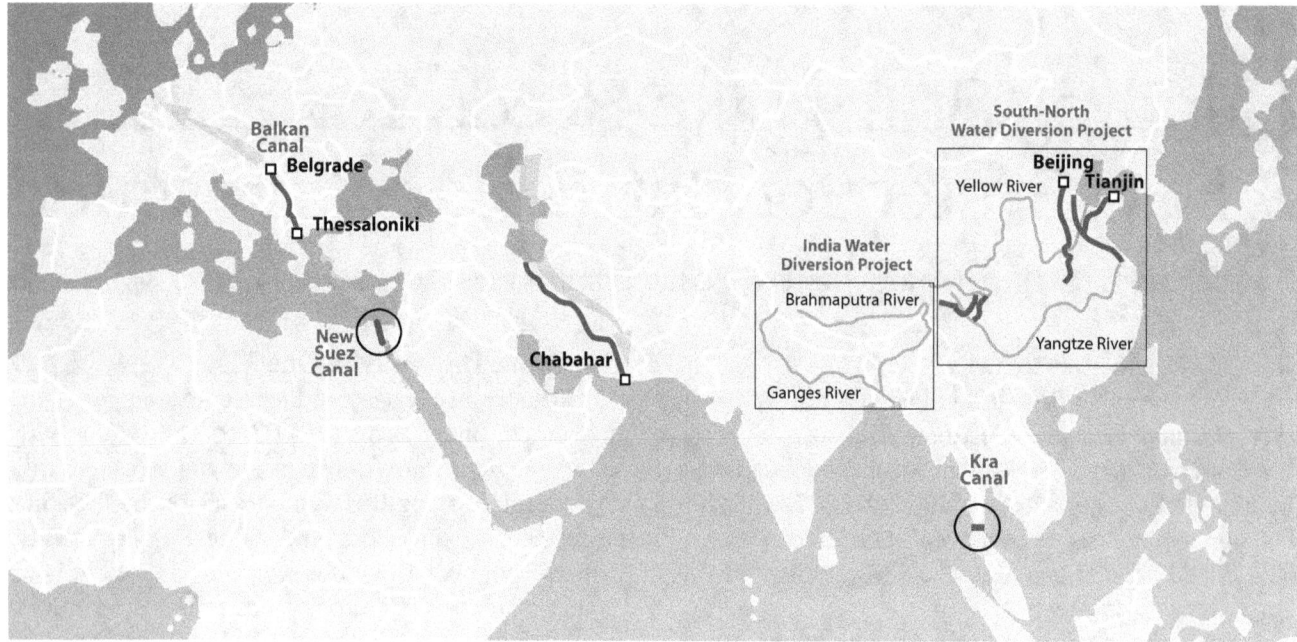

Yet, this escalated war danger is largely driven by the bankruptcy of the British Empire's dying economic system. Top bankers in London can only hope they survive the week. Regardless of the Brexit vote, the U.K., along with the entire trans-Atlantic financial system, is collapsing under the weight of massive speculation, fraud, and bankruptcy. Perhaps the EU will last one more week.

Africa remains ravaged from decades of post World War II neo-imperial destruction.

The nations of South America, many of which had shifted away from the trans-Atlantic death zone over the last five years, now face the consequences of London and Wall Street-directed coups which are intended to ensure their destruction, especially Argentina and Brazil. The coup against BRICS-proponent President Dilma Rousseff of Brazil has already been trumped by the corruption exposed among those who threw her out. Argentina faces brutal looting and destruction under the Obama and Wall Street-backed Macri. Mexico remains a Wall Street-controlled narco-state.

Now, consider the United States.

Following the attacks on 9/11, the United States has been under an ever more aggravated FBI-run police state, a state of perpetual war, and now one of increasing mass murders, record numbers of drug overdoses, depression-era real unemployment near 20%, and an increasing death rate as a result. For Obama to call this

an economic recovery, can only be termed satanic.

This system is done. The only option left is to flush Obama out with the sewage, and let Hillary and Trump go with him.

One more day, one more week,— this British Empire is finished and must be replaced.

A New System of Value For Long-Term Survival

Compare the desperation of the dying trans-Atlantic system, where any future existence depends on greater death-rates to maintain worthless speculative debts, to the growing Eurasian system.

China lifted over 600 million people out of poverty over 25 years. Over the coming 25 years, Asia will achieve far greater accomplishments, transforming what is already 60% of the world's population and 40% of world GDP, into the most vibrant economic sector in the world, even if only by virtue of the scientific optimism which is being achieved on such a broad scale.

It is the breadth and depth of vision of the projects which exemplify the new paradigm of development centered in the collaboration between Russia, China and India, which best expose the bankruptcy of the current trans-Atlantic program.

Take the Suez Canal in Egypt, which was expanded to double its width and double its annual capacity last year as part of the Maritime Silk Road. The plan estimated three years for completion, yet it took only one! So fast that most Americans blinked and are still unaware of the development. Compare this to the high-speed train in California, which under the current system would be lucky to build 100 km of rail line over the next twenty years, and plans to build only 600 km over the next fifteen years. China plans to build 11,000 km of high-speed rail in the next four years, giving it a total of 30,000 km.

One of the most revolutionary projects in modern history is another canal, one which is once again under active discussion. Opposed by the British Empire in the 19th Century because it would undermine the primacy of Singapore, a Crown entity, to control merchant trade from east Asia to south Asia, Africa, and Europe, the Kra Canal in Thailand would revolutionize trade among all nations of Asia, Africa, and Europe today, as well as establish an entirely new level of development in southeast Asia. The Kra Canal's estimated time for construction is currently ten years, but with the use of peaceful nuclear explosions (PNEs), would take only five.

A similar perspective exists for the proposed Persian Canal, from the new port at Chabahar to the Caspian sea, integrating all of central Asia into the Maritime Silk Road. Also, the proposed Balkan Canal, from Belgrade on the Danube to the Aegean port of Thessaloniki, Greece, would play a similar role. This would enable shipping to travel through the Suez Canal, into Belgrade and along the Danube River, through the Danube-Rhine Canal in Bavaria, all the way to Rotterdam on the North Sea Coast.

Consider then the critical question of water. India is embarking on a water diversion project to bring essential water supplies to both the south and east of the subcontinent. This project, to divert some of the Ganges and Brahmaputra waters, will require twenty years to build, transforming India's population of now over 1 billion persons. Plus, China will soon be embarking on the largest of its south-north water diversion projects in the coming years, completing the entire three-leg program over a twenty year period, eventually taking water from the Tibetan plateau to the areas around Beijing.

Yet, however impressive these projects are, this method of linear listing of projects remains insufficient to grasp the metric of growth now developing in Eurasia. They are too easily dismissed as simply infrastructure projects, though the scope of area (nearly 50% of

Krafft Ehricke envisioned the tasks for the exploration of our planetary system.

the world's land area), the accelerated rate of development, and the length of vision of these projects currently under construction, far surpasses anything mankind has ever seen.

The Higher Metric of Value

To grasp this higher metric of value, which lies outside statistical analysis, requires an extraterrestrial perspective. The demonstration of Einstein's notion of a physical space-time, beyond the mechanical constructs of a winding-down watch and Euclidean space, is found in the transformation of the human species generated by extended and sustained travel among the stars.

Before we achieve star travel, which remains a problem for coming generations, the task of exploration of our planetary system, as envisioned by Krafft Ehricke, sets the standard of increase or decrease in real, global economic value.

As of today, with China leading the way in collaboration with Russia, India, and even Europe, there are plans to achieve these goals in space exploration, most for the first time in history: a lander on the far side of the moon; a sample return from the moon; a manned landing on the far side of the Moon; a permanent lunar base; industrial mining of the moon. All this in addition to a new Chinese-built space station operational in 2020, continued advanced exploration of Mars, and asteroid defense technologies.

Yet, even beyond the clear investment returns,

which are irrefutable, as well as the technological advancements which are required to achieve the current objectives, the space program requires a non-linear transformation in human culture, as Krafft Ehricke emphasized in his work with Lyndon and Helga LaRouche.

Human culture cannot remain dominated by either a monetary metric, or by physical consumption levels. Mankind's total emergence from the physical restraints of poverty (fresh water, electricity, basic infrastructure, etc.) requires a new notion of value, beyond discrete statistical measurements. As German scientist Bernhard Riemann understood, the only metric of value sufficient within a system of non-linear transformations is one which is continuous, i.e. a metric

The German scientist and genius, Bernhard Riemann.

available only to the creative faculties of the human mind.

This is what all great geniuses have understood, and this, and only this, is the basis of a new economic system for the trans-Atlantic area, as well as the world and beyond. Based on the work of Riemann, Einstein, Krafft Ehricke, and Lyndon LaRouche, the new paradigm now burgeoning as a new geological epoch on our planet and beyond, will be a reality. As Brunelleschi's dome initiated the beginning of a new epoch in mankind's history, now known as the Italian Renaissance, so will the achievements towards mankind's emergence as an extra-planetary species be seen as the beginning of the greatest evolutionary leap in mankind's early beginnings.

The St. Petersburg Forum and The World of the Near Future

by Tony Papert

June 21—The June 16-18 St. Petersburg International Economic Forum (SPIEF) was a powerful and far-reaching intervention into every corner of the world. It was a unique event, unprecedented and unrepeatable. To those who are afraid to break away from Obama and the British Empire, it said: "Don't you realize what is possible for humanity now? Don't you realize what is being offered to you? Don't you see that you don't have to go to war with us? Here are the investments!"

The level of inspiration,— and fully justified inspiration,— which permeated it, is exemplified by this statement from Russian President Vladimir Putin's address there:

kremlin.ru

Russian President Vladimir Putin addressing the plenary session of the St. Petersburg International Econoomic Forum, June 17, 2016.

As early as June we, along with our Chinese colleagues, are planning to start official talks on the formation of comprehensive trade and economic partnership in Eurasia with the participation of the European Union states and China. I expect that this will become one of the first steps toward the formation of a major Eurasian partnership. We will certainly resume the discussion of this major project at the Eastern Economic Forum in Vladivostok in early September. Colleagues, I would like to take this opportunity to invite all of you to take part in it.

Friends, the project I have just mentioned—the greater Eurasia project—is, of course, open for Europe, and I am convinced that such cooperation may be mutually beneficial. Despite all of the well known problems in our relations, the European Union remains Russia's key trade and economic partner. It is our next-door neighbor, and we are not indifferent to what is happening in the lives of our neighbors, European countries and the European economy.

Look at the immediate sequels to the SPIEF. On June 23-24, Putin will join China's President Xi Jinping and Indian Prime Minister Narendra Modi at the Heads of State Summit of the Shanghai Cooperation Organization (SCO) in Tashkent, Uzbekistan. The current full members of SCO are China, Kazakstan, Kyrgyzstan, Russia, Tajikistan, and Uzbekistan, but both India and Pakistan are expected to be brought in as full members at this summit. Nor is that the end of it. "Iran is the next," said Uzbekistan President Nursultan Nazarbayev from St. Petersburg. "So, this organization with three billion residents is becoming a huge power," he added, according to PressTV.ir June 18, citing Interfax.

Xi and Putin will leave from that Tashkent meeting for a bilateral summit in China on June 25. Among the 30 agreements being prepared for their signature there, there is an emphasis on cooperation in space technology, as well as on great cross-border transpor-

The plenary session of the St. Petersburg International Economic Forum.

tation projects and energy. Russian Deputy Prime Minister Dmitry Rogozin, in charge of the Russian military-industrial and space complex, has been in China preparing the agreements on space exploration and defense.

A little further ahead, Japan's Prime Minister Shinzo Abe will attend the September meeting in Vladivostok mentioned by Putin as quoted above. There, not only is Japan to deepen its involvement in the economic level of the "greater Eurasia project," but it is actually possible that Putin and Abe will sign an agreement in Vladivostok which will settle the territorial disputes between Russia and Japan which have prevented the signing of a peace treaty between the two nations ever since the fighting stopped at the end of World War II.

Now the SPIEF occurred just as NATO, under Obama's orders, is preparing for imminent military aggression against Russia,— even if few have the courage to call it what it is. NATO is holding highly provocative military exercises all along Russia's western borders, assembling the biggest troop concentrations there since Hitler's preparations for his June 22, 1941 invasion,— exactly 75 years ago. A NATO summit of heads of government in early July is to jack up the provocations further. Will a war of annihilation be prevented? No one really knows yet.

But some have screwed up their courage. Germany's Foreign Minister Frank-Walter Steinmeier told Germany's mass-circulation *Bild am Sonntag* on June 19, "What we should not do now is inflame the situation further through saber-rattling and war cries. Whoever believes that a symbolic tank parade on the alliance's eastern border will bring security, is mistaken. We are well-advised not to create pretexts to renew an old confrontation." It would be "fatal to now narrow the focus to the military, and seek a remedy solely through a policy of deterrence." And just today, German Vice-Chancellor Sigmar Gabriel, from the same Social Democratic Party as Steinmeier, let it be known that he will travel to Moscow next Monday, June 27, to meet with Putin.

Big Role of South and Central America

As for the SPIEF sessions themselves, Europe was heavily represented, despite the sanctions. Italian Prime Minister Matteo Renzi met with Putin, and brought a very high-level business delegation, which is reported to have signed $1.4 billion in agreements with Russian companies. EU Commission President Jean-Claude Juncker was there, as was former French President Sarkozy and UN Secretary-General Ban Ki-moon. Six leaders of big German firms spoke in a panel on Ger-

kremlin.ru

Russian President Vladimir Putin (right) with Kazakstan President Nursultan Nazarbayev, May 8, 2016. At the St. Petersburg Forum, Nazarbayev said that the Shanghai Cooperation Organization, meeting June 23-24, is becoming a huge power.

man-Russian cooperation, along with EU Commissioner Günther Oettinger; Germany's top Russia expert, Alexander Rahr, was featured on another panel. A panel on Russian-Swiss cooperation included top corporate officials and an official of the Swiss Foreign Ministry; this occurred just as the Swiss government moved to withdraw the nation's 1992 application to join the EU, after a vote to that effect by both houses of the Swiss Parliament.

Some top Chinese businessmen were featured in the opening panels on the Group of 20 and another panel on China's "New Economic Model." A Russia-Africa panel included the President of Guinea and ministers from four other African nations. A Russia-Japan panel included six senior business executives and a vice-minister. A Panel on "Russia-India: A New Stage in Economic Partnership," included four top Indian executives. There was a BRICS panel with businessmen from every member nation; a Eurasian Economic Union panel; and a panel of the Shanghai Cooperation Organization (SCO) Business Forum. An Iran panel was titled, "Life After Sanctions: Re-Integrating Iran into the Global Economy."

The final panel was on "Russia-Bangladesh: An Era of New Opportunities." After the closing bell, there was a full-day conference on the development of the Arctic.

Forum organizer and Putin adviser Anton Kobyakov said that attendance had been about 12,000, and

that 1,300 companies had been represented.

The principal U.S. representative in St. Petersburg was the Chairman and CEO of ExxonMobil, Rex Tillerson.[1]

The vibrant exchange with South and Central America in St. Petersburg has been ignored in most U.S. and European accounts. In a June 16 interview with Sputnik, Ecuador's Minister of Knowledge and Human Talent, Andres Arauz, urged Ibero-American participants in the SPIEF to pay close attention to how China's New Silk Road, the BRICS Bank, and other new financial institutions are embarking on great projects to "change the history of civilization." South America must do the same, he said.

"We view with envy," Arauz said, "the great projects that change the history of civilization, with the New Silk Road that China has proposed to the world, the creation of the Asian Infrastructure Investment Bank (AIIB), the BRICS Bank, the Eurasian project which Russia defends … we are envious because, while South America proposed this ten years ago, we failed to consolidate it … We hope that the lessons posed at the St. Petersburg Forum can be applied to our region," Arauz told Sputnik. Russia, he said, is not only a trading partner, but "a strategic ally of Ecuador and the region."

Arauz is one of hundreds of government ministers and other officials from South and Central America and the Caribbean who attended the SPIEF, seeking greater economic and trade cooperation—as well as scientific and technological agreements—with Russia, China, and the nations of Asia, Africa, and Europe. The United States, under Barack Obama, offers them nothing except "green" technology, austerity, and depopulation.

In the course of the three-day SPIEF gathering, there were two seminars dealing with Ibero-America: "Russia-Latin American SMEs [Small and Medium-Sized Enterprises] as Catalysts in Building Value," and "Russia-Latin America: Foreign Trade and Investment Cooperation as Drivers of Economic Growth." The

_____

1. The program for the SPIEF is here.

President Vladimir Putin (left) shown meeting at the Kremlin with German Foreign Minister Frank-Walter Steinmeier, March 23, 2016.

kremlin.ru

panels included Russian speakers and representatives from Ibero-America and the Caribbean. Alexander Shchetinin, director of the Latin America Department at the Russian Foreign Ministry, told Nicaragua's *Radio Primerisima* that SPIEF will "open additional opportu-

nities to consolidate, above all, the economic relations among our countries."

There was more. On June 15, the day before SPIEF formally opened, it hosted a full-day panel on Latin American integration, including panels titled, "CARICOM and the Caribbean," "CAN—Andean Community," "SIECA—Central American Secretariat for Economic Integration," and "MERCOSUR," along with panels of Russian business and government representatives.

In another June 16 interview with RT, Uruguay's Vice President Raul Sendic, who had just spent three days in Moscow, echoed the same sentiment. "This relationship with Russia is good for America," he said. "Strengthening our relationship with Russia favors the balance of forces in the world, and opens to America, as well as to Russia, enormous opportunities."[2]

_____

2. The rationale and program of the June 15 "Latin America Interregional Forum, Trade and Investment" is here.

Xi Jinping's Strategic Mission to Central and Eastern Europe

by Mike Billington

June 21—In the Pacific, Obama's threatening patrols are flying and sailing close to Chinese territories, and are even deliberately violating Chinese sovereign territory at times. He is trying to build a web of Pacific alliances that will bring the United States to war with China in the Pacific. In Central and Eastern Europe, NATO is conducting provocative maneuvers on Russia's borders, gunning for war, as German Foreign Minister Frank-Walter Steinmeier has correctly implied.

And where was China's President Xi Jinping from June 17 to 21? In a strategic master-stroke worthy of Gen. William Tecumseh Sherman, Xi Jinping was precisely in Central and Eastern Europe, NATO's intended war front. Not on a mission of war, but a vital strategic mission subsuming the question of war,—one for a "win-win" policy of peaceful development, coordinated with Putin's St. Petersburg International Economic Forum.

China's President has been visiting Serbia in Eastern Europe, Poland in Central Europe, and Uzbekistan in Central Asia. Xi visited the Czech Republic in April, while Central and Eastern European (CEE) leaders have visited China this year. This diplomatic and economic cooperation is part of the 16+1 process established between China and the 16 CEE nations in 2012. Most of these nations were once part of the Soviet Union or the Warsaw Pact, while many now are part of the EU or are applying to join. The 16+1 thus serves as a crucial bridge between East and West, and in particular serves as the hub for developments along the New Silk Road connection between China and Europe.

Serbia has maintained strong relations with both Russia and China, even while it has been an applicant for membership in the European Union since 2007. Poland, on the other hand, under the current right-wing government, has fully joined Obama's mobilization for military confrontation with Russia. Poland is calling for permanent NATO bases, while installing U.S. missile systems on its soil, missiles which are a direct threat to Russian security. At the same time, Poland has very close ties with China. Xi Jinping's visit, expanding

Xinhua/Li Xueren

Chinese President Xi Jinping (left) shakes hands with his Russian counterpart Vladimir Putin in Ufa, Russia, July 8, 2015. Xi said that China and Russia should continue to maintain their high-level strategic coordination within the Shanghai Cooperation Organization.

Serbian government website http://www.srbija.gov.rs

Presidents Xi Jinping and Tomislav Nikolic of Serbia laying wreaths at the site of the former Chinese Embassy in Belgrade, destroyed by a U.S. bombing raid in 1999. The two Presidents later laid a cornerstone in the same location for the construction of a Chinese Cultural Center and unveiled a monument to Confucius.

their strategic relationship and economic ties, is a clear demonstration of the win-win policy followed by both China and Russia, encouraging cooperation in mutual economic development with all nations,— which simultaneously deprives Obama's puppets of their will to fight.

It is exemplary that Xi is following his Central and Eastern Europe tour with a visit to Uzbekistan, where the Shanghai Cooperation Organization (SCO) is holding its 16th annual Summit in Tashkent, and where he will meet with Russian President Vladimir Putin, who will then travel on to Beijing for a state visit to China.

Serbia: Meeting Place of East and West

In a signed article in Serbia's leading newspaper *Politika* on June 16, the day before his arrival, Xi Jinping wrote: "For centuries, Serbia has been a place where civilizations of the East and the West meet, interact and together bring about major progress in human civilization." He noted the close collaboration between the Chinese and Yugoslavia in fighting against "Fascist aggression on the Eastern and Western fronts in World War II," adding that Serbian President Tomislav Nikolic, in November 2015, attended the 70th anniversary celebration of victory in the "World Anti-Fascist War" in Beijing, "sending a strong message of our two countries' commitment to

upholding the post-war international order, safeguarding world peace, and building a better future for mankind."

Serbia is a major part of the New Silk Road, or the One Belt One Road (OBOR) as Beijing calls it,— referring to the overland New Silk Road Economic Belt and the 21st Century Maritime Silk Road by sea. China is already building major projects in and around Serbia, including the Belgrade-to-Budapest Railway, the Pupin Bridge over the Danube in Belgrade, and a roadway from Belgrade to Montenegro.

This was the first visit of a Chinese President to Serbia in 32 years, but the two nations signed a strategic partnership agreement in 2009, which has now been upgraded to a "Comprehensive Strategic Partnership." China has invested more than $1 billion in infrastructure and energy projects since then. None has been more important than the purchase in April of the 100-year-old Smedervo steel works by China's Hesteel Group, for euro 46 million, saving the company and its 5,000 workers from a probable shutdown. On June 19, Xi visited the steel company with President Nikolic and Prime Minister Aleksandar Vucic. "Let Chinese-Serbian cooperation set a good example for cooperation with other nations of Central and Eastern Europe," Xi said.

"Serbia holds an important, strategic position," President Nikolic said, adding that "Serbia is ready to become China's most important partner, and not only in the region. I am convinced that Serbia's future will look completely different from today."

The most dramatic moment of the visit came when Presidents Xi and Nikolic laid a wreath of white chrysanthemums at the site of the former Chinese Embassy in Belgrade, which was bombed and destroyed on May 7, 1999, by a U.S. B-2 stealth bomber, killing three Chinese.

Xi's wreath-laying did not indicate a desire for revenge—quite the opposite. Xi and President Nikolic laid a cornerstone at the site for the construction of a Chinese cultural center, and unveiled a monument to Confucius, as well as name plates for the newly named Confucius Street and the Square of Serbian-Chinese Friendship. There are already two Confucius institutes in Serbia, and Chinese is taught in over 100 middle and primary schools. To Xi, the Confucian concept of Harmony under Heaven applies to all people and all nations.

Assistant Prof. Milena Nikolic, daughter-in-law of President Nikolic, presented a proposal by herself and Dragan Duncic, for a Danube-to-Aegean Sea canal at the 30th Anniversary Schiller Institute Conference in 2014 in Germany.

As to Serbia's efforts to join the EU, Xi said he supports the bid.

China and Serbia also signed 21 agreements during the visit, in trade, infrastructure, and other fields. President Nikolic awarded President Xi Serbia's highest honor, the Grand Collar of the Order of the Republic of Serbia. Russian President Putin had received the same honor when he visited Belgrade in October 2014.

President Nikolic's daughter-in-law, Dr. Milena Nikolic, appeared in the official picture of Presidents Nikolic and Xi. In October 2014, she had presented Serbia's proposal for a canal between the Danube and the Aegean Sea—the Danube-Morava-Vardar/Axios-Aegean Waterway proposal—at a conference of Helga Zepp-LaRouche's Schiller Institute in Germany. China has since financed a feasibility study on the project, but it has not yet been released.

Serbia lies at a crucial point linking China's Silk Road Economic Belt and the 21st Century Maritime Silk Road. The Belt and the Road meet at the Greek port of Piraeus near Athens. In April, the China Ocean Shipping Company (COSCO) purchased a majority share of the port of Piraeus as the primary terminus of the 21st

Century Maritime Silk Road, for Chinese goods shipped to Europe. Goods going to Central and Eastern Europe will travel from Piraeus by rail—mostly built by China—through Macedonia, Serbia, Hungary, and on.

Poland: Silk Road and Amber Road

President Xi traveled on to Poland on Sunday, June 19. In an article published in the leading Polish newspaper, *Rzeczpospolita*, on June 17, Xi referred to Copernicus, Madame Curie, and Chopin as Poles who have made great contributions to mankind's progress, and who are well known and respected in China. He also noted the Polish Jesuit priest and scientist Michal Boym, who worked virtually alone to defend the last Ming Emperor in the 1640s against the Manchurian Qing invasion, and also published works on Asian flora and fauna.

Xi praised Poland's historic collaboration with China, as one of the first nations to recognize the People's Republic of China and the first Central European country to join the Asian Infrastructure Investment Bank (AIIB, initiated by China). China and Poland are each other's leading trading partners in their respective regions, with two-way trade of more than $17 billion in 2015. There are five Confucius institutes in Poland, and Xi said that a growing number of Chinese universities are teaching the Polish language.

He pointed out that Poland lies on both the Ancient Silk Road and the equally ancient Amber Road—so named when amber was the "gold of the north"—the north-south trade route from the Baltic region through Poland to Venice, and then on by ship. He noted that several Chinese rail routes to Europe either terminate in, or pass through Poland.

Xi indicated that Poland is pursuing reindustrialization, while China is seeking international cooperation in distributing "production capacity," a reference to his policy of using China's so-called excess capacity (in the context of the western economic collapse) to build industrial production facilities abroad.

Xi and President Andrzej Duda signed perhaps 40 deals and MOUs on June 20, mostly in construction, raw materials, energy, finance, and science. Duda said he hoped that Poland would be China's "gateway to Europe," pointing both to Gdansk Port and the land ports for the rail connections.

Xi and Duda went together to welcome a train arriving in Warsaw from China. Both were eating Polish apples—one of the agricultural products that can now be exported to China by rail. Polish freight group PKP Cargo operates 20 trains per week via the New Silk Road between Poland and China, each trip taking 11-14 days, twice as fast as ship and far cheaper than air.

Xi and Duda agreed to upgrade their relationship to a "comprehensive strategic partnership" from the existing strategic partnership, as Xi and Nikolic have also done for China and Serbia.

Xi made no public statements about Obama's military mobilization against Russia, nor about Poland's central role in the military encirclement of Russia, nor about the extreme danger of conflict leading to global thermonuclear war. However, in his article in *Rzeczpospolita* preceding his visit, Xi concluded with the following: "China and Europe need to follow the trend of the times for peace, development, and win-win cooperation. We should deepen strategic cooperation, increase communication and coordination on international affairs, and contribute to building a new type of international relations featuring win-win cooperation and a community of shared future for all mankind."

During President Xi Jinping's trip, he and Polish President Andrzej Duda admire Polish apples, which can now be exported to China via the New Silk Road trains connecting China and Europe.

Uzbekistan and the SCO

At the time of this writing on June 21, Xi has moved on to Uzbekistan in Central Asia for a state visit, at the invitation of President Islam Karimov, before attending the SCO Summit in Tashkent on June 23-24. In addition to meetings with government leaders, Xi will address Uzbekistan's Senate and the Legislative Chamber, the two houses of the Oliy Majlis.

The SCO Summit will officially accept both India and Pakistan as new SCO members, which now includes Russia, China, and four of the five Central Asian nations—Uzbekistan, Tajikistan, Kyrgyzstan, and Kazakstan. The addition of the two South Asia nations will mean that 60% of Eurasia will be collaborating through the SCO in both strategic and economic matters. There are concerns that the tensions and occasional hostilities between India and Pakistan may undermine the level of mutual political trust within the SCO, but both nations are anxious to join. The broader cooperation within the SCO could in fact contribute to resolving some points of contention between India and Pakistan.

Iran, which is now an observer at the SCO, is expected to be accepted as a member in the near future.

Cooperation between the SCO and the Eurasian Economic Union (EAEU), comprising Russia, Belarus, Kazakhstan, Armenia and Kyrgyzstan, provides a further basis for President Putin's call at the recent St. Petersburg International Economic Forum for a "Greater Eurasia," comprising potentially all of the Eurasian nations, including, Putin emphasized, the nations of the European Union.

This is the vision of the future, based on mutual development, both physical and cultural, which must be accomplished if the onrushing geopolitical warfare is to be prevented.

Time Is Ripe To Implement The Kunming Initiative

by Ramtanu Maitra

June 20—Regional collaboration among nations can create the opportunity to eradicate abject poverty. That is one of the operative principles in the Kunming Initiative for a transport corridor traversing extremely poor parts of India, Bangladesh, and Myanmar, and connecting them with major cities.

The political climate for cooperation to implement the Kunming Initiative—now known as the Bangladesh-China-India-Myanmar (BCIM) Economic Corridor—has greatly improved since China's President Xi and India's Prime Minister Narendra Modi have come to power. The corridor is a major part of the New Silk Road. It will link Kunming, the capital of China's thriving Yunnan province adjacent to Myanmar, with Kolkata—formerly called Calcutta by the British—a once great, eastern Indian port city that urgently seeks revival. It will pass through Mandalay in Myanmar and Dhaka, the capital of Bangladesh, as shown in **Figure 1**.[1]

A major segment of this route is the Burma Road—

1. The proposed BCIM Economic Corridor from Kunming to Kolkata might run via Chuxiong-Dali-Baoshan-Dehong (all in China's Yunnan province) to Namhkan-Lashio-Mandalay in Myanmar, Imphal in India's Manipur state, Silchar in India's Assam state, and Karimganj-Dhaka in Bangladesh. Namhkan is on the China-Myanmar border and Lashio is about 100 km south of Namhkan. Different versions of a free-trade area connecting Kunming and Kolkata have been floated for more than fifteen years. Discussions were often been stalled or abandoned due to unresolved Sino-Indian conflicts. See Ramtanu Maitra, "Three Eurasian Superpowers Forge New Deals for Security." *Executive Intelligence Review*, Nov. 1, 2013.

FIGURE 1

The Planned Route for the Bangladesh-China-India-Myanmar Economic Corridor

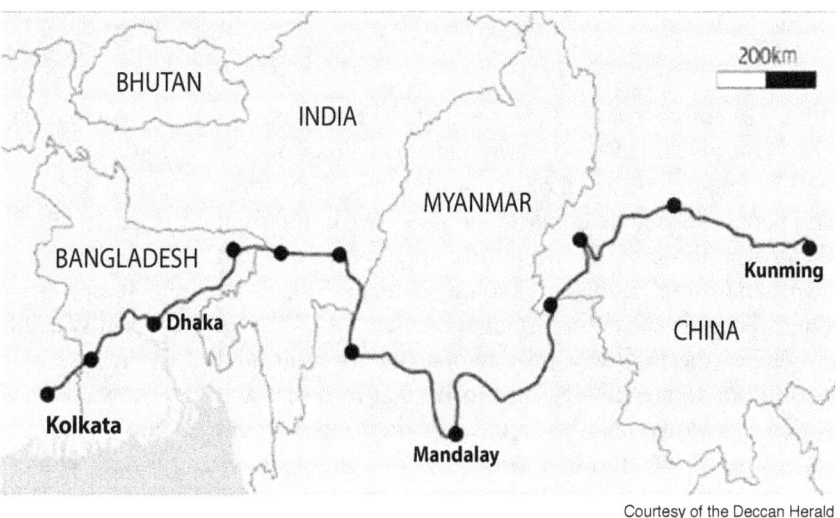

Courtesy of the Deccan Herald

from Lashio in Myanmar to Kunming in China, as shown in **Figure 2**—built by the British in 1937-1938 during the Second Sino-Japanese War to supply the Chinese, while Myanmar was still a British colony.

The BCIM project continues the process of breaking the isolation of Southeast Asia from South Asia, and South Asia's isolation from Central Asia and beyond, set in place by the British Empire and other imperial powers over more than two centuries.

The project involves upgrading sections of the existing 3,380 kilometer (2,100 mile) road and possibly also building high-speed rail from Kunming to Kolkata, as China has now proposed.

In January 2015, China proposed the high-speed rail line as part of the BCIM Economic Corridor. Li Jiming, Vice Secretary-General of Yunnan province, told In-

FIGURE 2
The Burma Road and the Stilwell (Ledo) Road

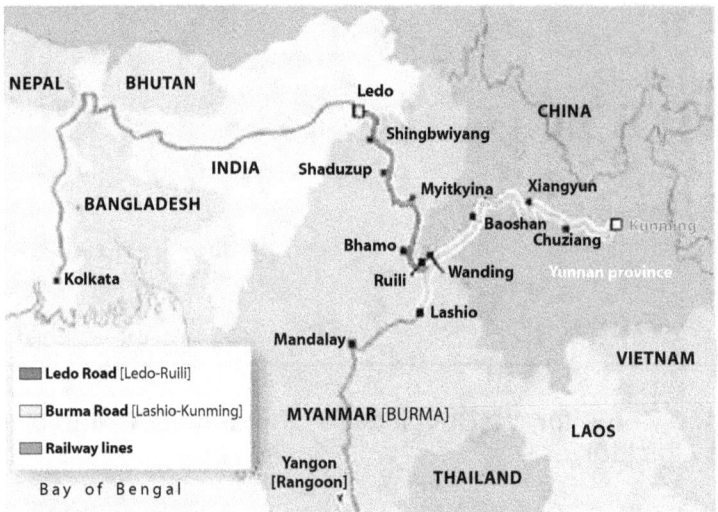

ments. But nothing was done; the governments were not interested. Now conditions have changed, and the engine is ready to rev up.

The project moved from back-channel talks to talks among the four governments at the first intergovernmental meeting held in December 2013. At that meeting, it was decided that each country would provide a country report on the Economic Corridor focusing on objectives of the corridor, scope and elements, principles and modalities of cooperation, and framework of co-operation. China, India, and Bangladesh have produced and shared their reports, but because of political uncertainty, Myanmar has lagged behind. All four reports are to be the basis of a single, agreed document at a meeting in Kolkata that has not yet been scheduled.

dia's *Economic Times*, June 18, 2015, "The proposal has been discussed with India and other countries. It will be beneficial for all of us as it will facilitate trade and people-to-people contact," he said. "We could fund the project through the Asian Infrastructure Investment Bank and other agencies," such as China's Silk Road Fund. There is as yet no formal agreement.

As for the highway, only two segments of around 200 kilometers each—Silchar to Imphal in India, and Kalewa to Monywa in Myanmar—are in need of urgent repair, according to Jin Cheng, Chief Counsel in the Foreign Affairs office of Yunnan province, in an interview with *The Hindu* June 16, 2016. The rest of the route is in fairly good condition, he said.

At present, those associated features that make a multimodal transport route into a true economic corridor—such as power production and transmission, water infrastructure, industrial development, and the building of new cities—are not part of the international planning, but are open to the planning of the individual governments.

Origins

Rehman Sobhan—an eminent Bangladeshi economist and founder of the Centre for Policy Dialogue in Dhaka—urged the development of multimodal transport along this route based on sound economic reasoning. In 1999, the first meeting of representatives from the four countries took place, hosted by the Yunnan Academy of Social Sciences, and the Kunming Initiative was born. These were largely not representatives of the govern-

Countervailing Winds

An earlier project—just to connect Myanmar to India—illustrates considerations that have sometimes prevented governments from embracing such corridors. In 2005, Indian and Chinese survey teams began mapping out plans to rebuild the Stilwell Road, named in honor of U.S. General "Vinegar Joe" Stilwell of World War II fame and built with a large contribution of African American troops in a multi-national effort (shown as the Ledo Road in Figure 2). China did all of the reconstruction work, paving dozens of miles with granite stones packed into earth. India, however, did not move. Why?

Observers have offered several reasons for India's reluctance at the time. Much of India's northeastern region—through which the road winds its way into Bangladesh—had been made unstable by the secessionist Naga tribes with backing from foreign NGOs and British intelligence. New Delhi feared that rebuilding the road would ease the way for these hostile forces, including drug smugglers, to enter India's troubled area to fan the flames. There were also fears that the Chinese, who had earlier aggressively sought to take over trade in Myanmar, would "use" the Stilwell Road to also flood the markets in the northeastern region of India. (But what about the large amount of trade that was already going from India to China?)[2]

2. Additional insights into the dimensions of resistance are provided in Ramtanu Maitra, "Prospects Brighten for Kunming Initiative," *Asia Times*, Feb. 12, 2003.

Courtesy of Ge Shuya

The "24-zig," a segment of the Burma Road in China. China plans to get rid of the kinks—with high-speed rail.

Why the Time Is Now Ripe

But now is the time for the BCIM Economic Corridor. Chinese investors are gearing up to join India's "Make in India" campaign by setting up factories in West Bengal, according to Kong Can, Deputy Director-General of the Yunnan Development Research Center, a think tank in Kunming, in an interview in *The Hindu* June 16, 2016. "We wish to become partners in Prime Minister Narendra Modi's 'Make in India' campaign by investing in this project," Kong said. Yunnan province

has autonomous status and can make these decisions on its own.

Kong's statements reflect China's interest in investing abroad, now widely known. But this major development by itself would not have provided the Kunming Initiative the necessary boost, if other regional developments had not begun to take shape. For instance, two major economic corridor developments have been announced in recent months that link up a number of countries of the region.

China is in the process of developing the China-Pakistan Economic Corridor, which will link the city of Kashgar in Xinjiang province to Pakistan's Gwadar Port on the Arabian Sea, running through Pakistan from north to south.

Equally important is the May 23 agreement between Iran, India, and Afghanistan to develop Chabahar Port in Iran and to make Chabahar an industrial hub. India will invest close to $20 billion in the industrial hub and will also finance the development of the port itself. This undertaking—and the associated transport corridor that will run close to Iran's juncture with Afghanistan and Pakistan—when completed, will provide Afghanistan efficient access to the sea and to the wider world for the first time. The port and the corridor will also enable India and the Indian Ocean littoral states to access not only Iran, Afghanistan, and Central Asia by sea and land, but also to access Russia and Europe further west.

These two major developments signal the breakdown of the isolation of Southeast Asia, South Asia, and Central Asia from each other, progressively set in place especially by the British Empire, over the last 200 years and more. To make that breakthrough, what was needed was the rise of China and India as formidable economic powers, seeking to spread their capabilities across Asia. Even Asia's island nations in the Far East, such as Japan, and the "island" nation of South Korea, have begun to move west to join this development process.

Developments in the BCIM Region

For the region of the BCIM economic corridor, perhaps the most important milestone was the April 2014 agreement between China and India to establish a "strategic and cooperative partnership for peace and prosperity." These two most populous Asian nations, both economic giants, were already in close collaboration on the world stage, being members of the BRICS and of the associated banks that are oriented to infrastructure development. Now, with India and Pakistan becoming full members this month of the Shanghai Cooperation Organization (SCO)—which already includes China and Russia—the collaborating mechanisms are growing stronger.

On the ground in South Asia, other major changes have taken place, or are in the process of taking place. Myanmar—at the junction between South Asia, China, and Southeast Asia—is now emerging from its isolation and stagnation after decades of military rule. The new government could play a major role by utilizing Myanmar's junction status to mobilize the BCIM project.

Meanwhile, developments between India and Bangladesh hold promise for unprecedented economic gains through new, multimodal connections. There have been decades of virtual stagnation in bilateral relations, resulting from the walls erected by the British Raj's departing ugly kick that divided the subcontinent and killed millions. Bangladesh had been carved out of India; and India, which surrounds Bangladesh on three sides, was left with a very long route "up and around" for travel between peninsular India and its easternmost states. But on Nov. 1, 2015, after signing of an agreement, a cargo vehicle carrying a car and goods made the first successful trial run from Kolkata *through Bangladesh* to Agartala, capital of the Indian state of Tripura, reviving a route closed since the ugly kick at Independence in 1947 and cutting the travel distance by a thousand kilometers.

The trial run came four-and-a-half months after South Asian transport ministers signed, on June 15, 2015, the landmark Bangladesh, Bhutan, India, Nepal (BBIN) Motor Vehicles Agreement for the Regulation of Passenger, Personnel, and Cargo Vehicular Traffic among their countries.

"Nearly seven decades after Partition, trains are set to run from Kolkata to Agartala through Bangladesh," Samudra Gupta Kashyap reported in the *Indian Express* Nov. 30, 2015. Kashyap added, with arithmetic irony, "India is building a 10 billion rupee [about $150 million], 15 km railway line connecting Agartala with Akhaura in Bangladesh. The line … is expected to be completed by 2017, and cut the distance between Agartala and Kolkata to 499 km from the existing 1,590 km route via Badarpur, Lumding, Guwahati and New Jalpaiguri."

India's 'Look East' Policy

But of course, as the BBIN agreement indicates, it is not all about efficiently connecting one part of India with another. In early January of this year, Nirmala Sitharaman, one of India's Ministers of State, speaking at Srimantapur in western Tripura state along the Bangladesh border, said: "The Indian government led by Prime Minister Narendra Modi is keen to develop all types of connectivity with all neighboring countries, including Bangladesh, to boost trade, economy, and people-to-people relations … The government has taken steps to develop road, rail, water, and air connectivity with the neighboring countries. With good physical linkages, India wants to further develop all types of relations with the adjoining countries."

This is a clear statement of what India has long been projecting, a "look east" policy, conceived in the early 1990s, which has now become a priority. Sithamaran was in Srimantapur to inaugurate an Integrated Development Complex for the India-Bangladesh border, that has modern facilities for customs and immigration, a banking and currency exchange facility, a warehouse, and public utility services.

India now proposes to expand its maritime trade by developing Bangladesh's Payra Port in the Ganges-Brahmaputra Delta. India Ports Global—a joint venture of state-run Jawaharlal Nehru Port Trust (JNPT) and Kandla Port—has shown interest after Payra Port invited proposals for its development from global companies, according to the Indian Ministry of Shipping. "Talks are on between our foreign ministry and [Bangladesh]. Dhaka also wants us. We have sent a team there for studies," said India's Shipping Minister Nitin Gadkari, a key negotiator for Chabahar Port with Iran, according to PTI.

Myanmar will also have port development. At the end of 2015, China's CITIC Group Corporation—together with four other Chinese companies and one from Thailand—formed two consortia that won their bid to build a deep-sea port in Myanmar's planned Kyaukpyu Special Economic Zone on the Bay of Bengal. The port is designed to have a handling capacity of 7.8 million tons of cargo and 4.9 million twenty-foot-equivalent units of containers. "With access to the Indian Ocean, Myanmar borders China and India—the two countries with the largest populations in the world," said Yuan Shaobin, a representative of CITIC Consortium, according to *China Daily Asia* on April 1. He added, "The country has a strategically important location and huge market potential in the region."

II. The British, the Saudis and the FBI

It's the Same People Who Brought You 9/11

by Jeffrey Steinberg

June 20—The initial Obama-mainstream-media fairy-tale that the Orlando mass killing was the work of the Islamic State has rapidly disintegrated, as new evidence points to the very same combination of forces that carried out the original 9/11 attacks—the British, the Saudis, and the FBI—the same combination that later created ISIS in the first place.

In classical intelligence parlance, such operations are known as "false flags."

Orlando mass murderer Omar Mateen was a longtime employee of one of the biggest and nastiest of the British Crown's private security agencies—G4S, with 620,000 employees in over 100 countries. G4S is the third-largest private corporation in the world, and it is a critical part of the British Monarchy's "invisible empire" of private mercenaries, assassins, and clandestine operatives. In the United States, G4S has security contracts for 90% of the nation's nuclear power plants, is a major sub-contractor for the Department of Homeland Security, and even handled the security for the British Petroleum offshore oil rigs in the Gulf of Mexico, which is where Omar Mateen worked for a number of years.

Despite the fact that co-workers demanded Mateen's firing because of his psychotic and violent behavior, the firm kept him on, and arranged for him to get a concealed-weapon license.

U.S. District Court Judge Colleen McMahon stated in court, in the case of the Newburgh Four FBI sting, that

"... there would have been no crime here, except the government instigated it, planned it and brought it to fruition."

It has emerged, in the wake of the Orlando massacre, that G4S lied in its claims that Mateen had been successfully put through psychological evaluation. The doctor whose name appeared in his file told reporters that she never met Mateen—and was not even working for G4S at the time of his supposed psychological evaluation. G4S dismissed the discrepancy as a "clerical error."

Mateen made two trips to Saudi Arabia, in 2011 and 2012, staying in four-star hotels and other high-end accommodations. It is not known what he was doing there, although both trips took place while he was employed by G4S. The second trip involved a group of New York City law enforcement officers and students from New York University.

For almost a year, Mateen was under FBI investigation for suspected terrorist ties, but ultimately, the Bureau dropped the case and at no time was his job with G4S in jeopardy. The FBI "investigation" involved the use of wiretaps, other electronic surveillance, informants and, at one point, an undercover effort to entrap him in a terrorist plot.

FBI's Jihadist Army

In fact, recent reports in the *New York Times* and *The Intercept* online publication make clear that the FBI, itself, has been running an army of paid "Islamist" provocateurs, run through the classic FBI "sting" operations made famous in the

1970s and '80s Operation Abscam and Brilab, in which FBI agents were disguised as rich Arab sheikhs, to lure Members of Congress and the labor movement into entrapments. Half of all of the so-called "terrorism" cases opened by the FBI since 9/11 involved these sting techniques, and in many cases, the targets were mentally ill, or financially desperate, or both.

According to theantimedia.org, of the 508 terrorism cases opened by the FBI since 9/11, 243 involved FBI informants, almost all of whom were Muslims, and many suffered from diagnosed mental illnesses. Many were desperate for money and were susceptible to bribery by the FBI to join alleged terror plots that were actually sting operations. The Newburgh Four case is highlighted in the story, which is based, in part, on a 2014 study by the Coalition to Protect Civil Freedoms, "Inventing Terrorists: Lawfare of Pre-emptive Prosecutions."

One of the four defendants in that case, James Cromitie, was an ex-drug addict and repeatedly rejected the offers of money from FBI undercover agents to participate in the terror plot. A second defendant, Laguerre Payan, was diagnosed with schizophrenia, and a third, David Williams, was desperate for money because his brother needed a life-saving liver transplant.

Another case, involving Rezwan Ferdaus, was an even more blatant case of FBI targetting of a mentally ill person. Ferdaus was suffering from severe depression, to the point that he could not control his bladder, but was pushed by the FBI into joining an FBI-manufactured plot to attack the Capitol Building.

In another case cited in the theantimedia.org story of June 15, a Boston father alerted the FBI when his son was posting on Facebook in favor of ISIS, and the FBI stepped in and provided the boy with weapons, and then busted him. Another prime case was that of Sam Osmakac. Osmakac was given weapons by the FBI, was instigated by an FBI informant, was provided with a car bomb by the FBI, and was given money to pay his travel costs to the site where he was eventually arrested. A court-ordered psychiatric exam revealed that he had schizoaffective disorder. His FBI case officer called him "a retarded fool."

Former FBI Assistant Director Thomas Fuentes described this as the FBI's policy of "Keep Fear Alive" to assure continuing expanded budgets. In reality it is a lot worse than just budget motivation, as the role of the FBI in the cover-up of 9/11 illustrates most clearly.

The same profile of the FBI creating terrorism where it does not exist, via sting operations, appeared in a lengthy piece in the *New York Times* on June 7, 2016,

under the headline "FBI Steps Up Use of Stings in ISIS Cases." *Times* reporter Eric Lichtblau reported that two-thirds of the FBI's terrorism prosecutions are based on stings, a significant increase in recent years. The *Times* story cited the case of the Newburgh Four, quoting Judge Colleen McMahon, who declared in court that "I believe beyond a shadow of a doubt that there would have been no crime here, except the government instigated it, planned it and brought it to fruition." An earlier *New York Times* article on April 28, 2012, headlined "Terrorist Plots, Hatched by the F.B.I." made the same case of FBI entrapment creating terrorism that would never have otherwise materialized.

Another FBI sting operation was reported on Feb. 26, 2015, in *The Intercept* online journal by Glenn Greenwald, who poignantly described it as "another FBI victory over the mentally ill."

Anglo-Saudi-FBI Nexus

If you want to understand how the British control and manipulate American politics, just carefully study this Anglo-Saudi-FBI nexus. It is this apparatus—which has been a dominant factor since the 1985 launching of the Anglo-Saudi Al-Yamamah oil-for-weapons deal, with its offshore secret accounts to bankroll global jihadi terrorism—that must be fully exposed and crushed if the United States is to ever regain its independence.

This is why the British, the Saudis and the FBI are terrified about the prospect of the release of the 28-page chapter from the original Joint Congressional Inquiry into 9/11. The evidence contained in those pages—regardless of the lies of John Brennan and Barack Obama—opens the window on the entire top-down British Empire control over global terrorism. The just-filed H.Res.779,— demanding the immediate publication of the 28-page chapter from the Joint Congressional Inquiry into 9/11 in the Congressional Record, with no Obama or John Brennan interference, under the Constitutional separation of powers,— is a powerful intervention. The introduction of the bill on the day that the Saudi Deputy Crown Prince and power behind the throne, Prince Mohammed bin Salman, arrived in Washington to meet with John Kerry, Ashton Carter, John Brennan, James Clapper, Paul Ryan, and Nancy Pelosi, is perfect timing.

This is a showdown moment, and every sane force must be mobilized to force out the truth about the British-Saudi Empire, and to bring down that Empire, with its Wall Street/FBI appendage, once and for all.

EDITORIAL

If They Heard It, They Didn't Understand It

During the June 18 session of the Manhattan Dialogue, moderator Dennis Speed asked John Sigerson, the Music Director of the Schiller Institute, to respond to a question on the sense of urgency, and the sense of responsibility that is required from Congressmen, and that we require from ourselves.

John Sigerson: Let me attempt to put a fine point on what Dennis was just saying. If the people who were at that nightclub—anybody who was at that nightclub, or anybody who goes to Disney World, and so forth, even if they knew,— maybe they've heard the Mozart *Requiem*,— they haven't really understood it. What I would say, is that once you *understand* and you actually *live* the Mozart *Requiem* and the Classical culture that was characterized by these individuals, these incredibly creative individuals like Mozart and Beethoven—who were very political, by the way—then emotionally, these things, these kinds of degraded activities, gambling, going to nightclubs, all these kinds of things,— "entertainment" in general,— just really becomes rather meaningless emotionally to one.

One is, rather, *gripped* by something which I would like to say is a *purpose*. And the problem today with a lot of people who attempt to delve into so-called "Classical" music, is that much of the Classical music

that's been done, especially since the death of the great German conductor Wilhelm Furtwängler, a lot of the Classical music that's been done since then, has lacked that purpose.

Rather, it has been a form of refined "entertainment" for the people who like to feel good, to go home from a concert "feeling good" in one way or another. And so, in a certain way, it's a kind of refined nightclub experience for a lot of people.

When we founded the Schiller Institute,— I was a founding member in 1984 with Helga Zepp-LaRouche,— one of the included intents of the Schiller Institute, was to change that and to return to a real

A bust of Wolfgang Amadeus Mozart, in Bratislava, Slovakia.

Library of Congress

Ludwig van Beethoven

idea of Classical culture. Now, when I say "Classical" maybe some people might be confused, so let me just use a way of putting that, that Lyndon LaRouche frequently would like to do.

In contrasting the Romanticism of, say, a Richard Wagner, to the Classicism of, say, a beautiful Beethoven symphony, he would say that with Wagner, you don't "leave a dry seat in the house." As opposed to with Beethoven, you don't "leave a dry eye in the house."

That really is it: Because Classical does not mean a period of music, and a period of time— you know, you had the Baroque, and you had the Classical, and then you had the post-Classical, and then you have the Romantic, all this stuff. That's meaningless. "Classical" is an idea; it's a concept; it's a principle. It's a principle of a way of thinking, which is why this question of Einstein comes up.

One of the ways that Einstein would figure things out, is once he reached a certain kind of impasse in his thinking, in his working out of problems, he would put down whatever he was writing, his writing implements, and whatever he was working on; and he would pick up his violin. And he would play, usually Bach, but also Mozart as well. And that was the way he would be able to work these paradoxes through.

Because one of the things about Classical

From a print in the British Museum

Johann Sebastian Bach (1685-1750), German musician and composer, shown here playing the organ, circa 1725.

Steve Carr

A statue of Friedrich Schiller in Detroit, Michigan.

music that's different than any other kinds of music, is that it implicitly poses a paradox, which in order for you to solve, you have to have an idea of a purpose. And as Schiller pointed out, in a lot of his aesthetic writings, when you do a concert or something like that, any kind of event, you have failed if you just send people back, "feeling good," and feeling just sort of "elevated."

We went to one of these events just the other day, of the "Big Sing" up there at St. John the Divine. And we sang a lot of good music there, with this huge—how big was that chorus? Four or five hundred people there, singing. This was part of the Choral Consortium, and it was a lot of not bad music, including some Bach pieces. There were certain platitudes that were said by each of the conductors about Orlando and so forth. But clearly, the people left there, by and large,— outside of the people whom *we* talked to about the idea of doing a memorial for 9/11,— outside of that, most people just went, having that "warm, fuzzy feeling."

Let me talk about the *Requiem* just a little bit: The first time that we performed the *Requiem* was shortly after the Schiller Institute was founded, in 1984. In October 1984, the Prime Minister of India, Indira Gandhi, whom both Lyndon and Helga had met with and were friends with, was assassinated. Since then, it has always been my intent, and our intent, never to do a *Requiem* just for the sake of doing a piece of music. A *Requiem* is a very special kind of celebration of the life of the individual, and the life of the individual after his mortal remains have passed. And you need to focus on an individual, and in that case it was Indira Gandhi, and we did that, and we really freaked people out when we did that.

For many of the enemies of the LaRouche movement, the FBI, people who were dedicated to stopping everything that LaRouche represented,— this was a last straw. Shortly after that, many of the real attacks and the legal attacks and jailings and frameups occurred in the late 1980s and 1990s, which sent Mr. LaRouche and many of our associates to jail for a number of years.

We're past that. But, we continue to think about and to rebuild that idea of the Mozart *Requiem* as a very important instrument for the uplifting of human beings, to give them an idea of what it really means to be human.

So, once you leave a concert, if it's successful, you leave the concert having made a decision to change. If you haven't decided to change, if the concert has not changed you— nowadays, people say they're "moved," but really, what does that mean? If you're really moved, you're moved *to change*, to change the way you think, to reject something that may have been

EIRNS/Stuart Lewis

Indira Gandhi at the National Press Club in Washington, D.C., July 30, 1982.

very dear to you, but you realize it's inferior, and therefore you have to get rid of it, like smoking or something, or drugs, or something else that you have to give up, because you've found that there's something higher, something more important.

The second time we did the Mozart *Requiem* I think was two and half years ago, in Boston. Again, this had a great purpose, which was the memorializing of [the 50th anniversary of] the assassination of John F. Kennedy. And it was really quite remarkable, at that time, because we found that *nobody else* was doing anything about this! There was nobody else who really was saying—I mean there were a couple of people saying a few things, but nobody was really celebrating who Kennedy *was*, and what he represented, and the kind of *hope* that he represented, for developing the *entire world*, the entire world economy. And that was a very successful concert that we gave up in Boston at the Holy Cross Cathedral, to a full audience of 1,200.

We also did a performance of it around that same time in northern Virginia, which was also quite interesting, because of various—and we decided *not* to do it right inside Washington, D.C., when we found we had a much better response outside of Washington (surprise, surprise!).

We are now in the process of putting together something which is yet bigger, which is a series of

Franklin D. Roosevelt Library

Eleanor Roosevelt and Presidential Candidate John F. Kennedy in New York, Oct. 11, 1960.

concerts of the Mozart *Requiem*, one after the other, over the series of days over the weekend of 9/11, which is the 15th anniversary of 9/11. 9/11 happens to be itself, falling on a Sunday, and we are going to be performing the *Requiem* as part of a celebratory Mass at a major church.

But we're also going to be having performances in almost every other borough in New York on other days around that time. That's the intent.

And the other intent to do it, is as I said, in a way that's not just celebrating—it's going to be political, in the way that we're talking about. That is, there's no way, nowadays, especially with what's happened in Orlando, and what's going on with the 28 pages, and the incredible fight that's now bursting out in Congress—there's no way that you can say that these things are apolitical. I mean, hopefully,— let us hope that by the time we do that performance on 9/11, Obama will have already been gone. That would be a very good celebration.

I encourage those people who have not participated with our chorus, to participate. We are openly inviting people to join in and work on the Mozart *Requiem* over this Summer. We have many people whom we've met over the last few weeks, who are very interested in coming in, maybe even bringing their whole choruses in. So we could end up with a quite large chorus, as long as people come to the rehearsals, so that they can actually do it properly.

I think that's what I want to say right now. It's going to be a really big deal, doing these, and it's going to make an *incredible* impact, through the metropolitan area and around the world as far as I can see. Because we're going to be doing the only thing—I mean, there will probably be other very emotional ceremonies, going on on 9/11. But I think what we're doing is going to raise that to the highest level, which is what we have to do, so that we really give meaning to the lives of *every single human being's life,* who was slaughtered on that day 15 years ago.